P I L G … E

EXETER

David Ison

Illustrated by
Jean Hall and Joy Yeates

CANTERBURY
PRESS
Norwich

First published in 1999 by The Canterbury Press Norwich
(a publishing imprint of Hymns Ancient & Modern Limited
a registered charity)
St Mary's Works, St Mary's Plain
Norwich, Norfolk NR3 3BH

British Library Cataloguing in Publication Data

A catalogue record for this book is available
from the British Library

ISBN 1-85311-250-X

Typeset by Rowland Phototypesetting Ltd,
Bury St Edmunds, Suffolk IP32 6NU
Printed and bound in Great Britain by
Redwood Books, Trowbridge, Wilts

Contents

EXETER CATHEDRAL

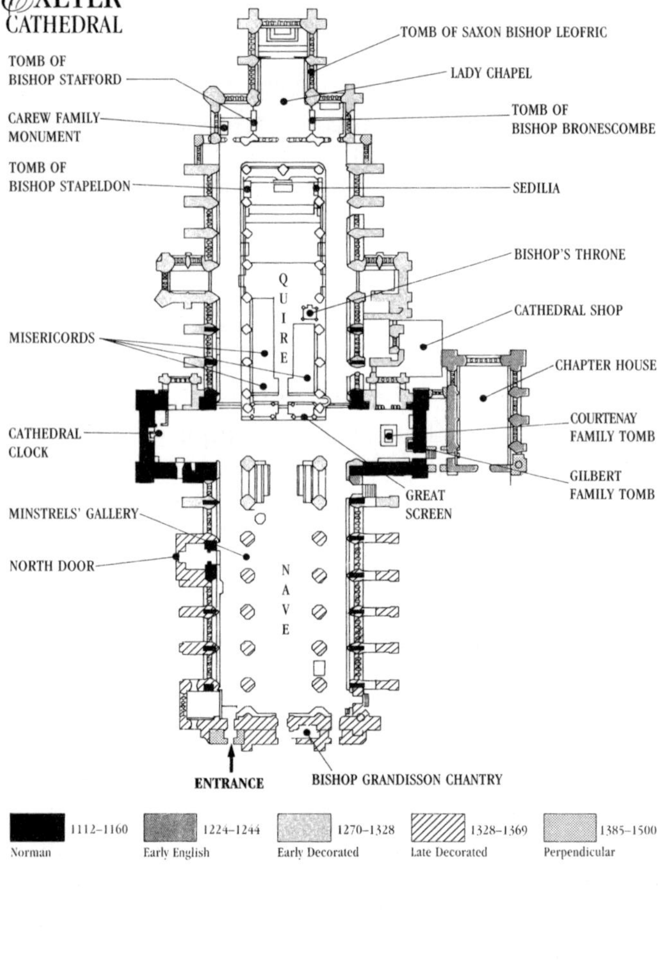

Introduction

The Romans began the building of Exeter. At the centre of their settlement here they set up a bath-house and a meeting-place. It is likely that their Christian successors had a church somewhere in the city, and it is certain that the Saxons had a minster church just to the west of the present Cathedral. When Leofric became Bishop of Crediton and St Germans in 1049, he united these two poor sees and moved the bishop's seat to the minster in Exeter, which by then was a walled and reviving city. After the upheaval of the Norman Conquest, the Conqueror's nephew, Bishop William Warelwast, in 1114 began building a new and grand Cathedral, with unique twin towers. This Norman Cathedral ended in a semicircular apse about where the Bishop's throne now stands. Its towers had largely solid walls at either side and acted as chapels rather than open transepts.

So although the Cathedral was the same width as it is today, it had less space inside it. When the new Salisbury Cathedral was completed in 1258, the Exeter clergy looked longingly at the extra space that it had, and they noted how suitable it was for elaborate processions, and so plans were laid to rebuild the Cathedral at Exeter. The Lady Chapel was begun in about 1270 under Bishop Walter Bronescombe, and the Cathedral was gradually demolished and rebuilt westwards from there. However, the towers and the bases of the Nave walls were kept, and new walls, a new roof and new windows were put on top, and the inside walls of the towers were demolished to form the transepts. The ceiling is the greatest glory of the building. It is the longest Gothic ceiling in the world, uninterrupted by a central tower. The Nave was substantially completed by 1342 under Bishop Grandisson, and the West Front, with its statues, was added after that. The Cathedral has remained structurally the same ever since, although there have been some modifications in detail. Thankfully, the wall built across the middle by the victorious dissenters in the English Civil War didn't last long!

The building you see is unique, and yet it has a family resemblance to other cathedrals. It is worship in stone. It expresses its builders' longing and reaching out for God (as well as more mixed motives, such as keeping up with ecclesiastical fashion and showing the importance of the city and its bishop). Many people have had a hand in its construction: Master Roger and Thomas of Witney, master masons; generous bishops and benefactors; many ordinary people who gave money; many workmen who gave their labour; in more recent times, Gilbert Scott, who carried out restoration work; and Herbert Read and others, who did heroic rebuilding work after the last War.

The Christian faith itself is built on the shared experience and witness of generations of saints, great and small, famous and unknown. When Exeter Cathedral was made there was a much greater awareness than there is now of a living community worshipping God throughout time as well as space. This *Pilgrim Guide* reflects this in its text and authorship. It was written in 1998 by the four members of the Cathedral Chapter: the Dean, Keith Jones; the Treasurer, Arthur Mawson; the Precentor, Kenneth Parry; and the Chancellor, David Ison. No one has a full grasp of the whole truth, whether of our Cathedral or of the faith to which it witnesses. Our intention has been to share with you something of our shared pilgrimage of faith in this place.

Prayers

Too late I have come to love you,
O Beauty of long ages past.
You were inside me,
and I was outside looking for you there.
You were with me, but I was not with you.

St Augustine

O Christ my Master and Lord,
grant that I may know you more clearly,
love you more dearly,
follow you more nearly,
day by day.

St Richard of Chichester

✠

From the statues of the West Front to the glass figures of the great East Window, we invite you to come on a pilgrimage through one of the loveliest cathedrals of England, in the company of the saints.

The West Front

We begin where medieval pilgrims started, standing outside the West Front of the Cathedral, looking at the image screen. This was added to the front of the building during the hundred years from 1340, and is surpassed only by Wells Cathedral in scale. When it was first made, it was painted in bright colours, and shone out as a beacon to guide travellers to its doors. Now only traces of paint are left. The figures are worn, but their majesty remains.

Here are people carved in different ages, from medieval to modern. Here in serried ranks are representatives of biblical writers and apostles, warriors and kings, angels and saints, centred on the divine figure above the Great West Door. As you come into this house of God, you are reminded that you do not come alone. Pilgrimage is not an individual activity, but, like all Christian prayer, is shared with others on earth and in heaven – the living and the departed, 'the quick and the dead'. You may notice that the figures have been damaged by the weather and have also been jumbled together by the activities of different ages. Thus a statue of Richard II sits at the right hand of God (or is it a figure of Christ?) in the centre of the screen, owing to an early nineteenth-century

The outside of the Great West Door

mix-up. So we come to God with our own mixed and marred lives, which nevertheless are still precious in God's sight. As real and fallen people we can nonetheless come to God through Christ, our Saviour.

Bishop Grandisson

To the right of the Great West Door you can see at ground level the small windows of the chantry chapel which Bishop John Grandisson had made for his tomb. Grandisson presided over the completion of the Cathedral, and died in 1369 after forty-two years as Bishop. His tomb was robbed a century after his death, but a beautiful gold ring was left behind which is now on display in the Cathedral Library.

Most important clergy and nobles in the Middle Ages wanted to be buried near to the High Altar, the most holy place in the Cathedral. John Grandisson wanted to lie at the door instead. The image screen is more his memorial, perhaps, than a plain tomb; but his position both guards and invites those who come to the Cathedral door. So may we, with our mixed motives and physical frailty, help those whom we meet to enter into the reality of God's presence. And Grandisson's tomb also reminds us that none of us is indispensable: one day we will all have to let go of the responsibilities and position that we have in life, and lay down before our own mortality.

The ring of Bishop Grandisson

Prayer

O God, make the door of this house wide enough
to receive all who need human love and fellowship;
narrow enough to shut out all envy, pride and strife.
Make its threshold smooth enough
to be no stumbling-block to children, nor to
straying feet,
but rugged and strong enough
to turn back the tempter's power.
God, make the door of this house
the gateway to your eternal kingdom.

Thomas Ken

At the apex of the West Front is the figure of St Peter, the patron saint of the Cathedral. The original figure was majestic, like the one in the West Window of Peter, the first Bishop of Rome. Its replacement, carved by Simon Verity in 1984, shows the man as he was: stripped naked for fishing, the Peter of impetuous heart and fearful denial, a human being forgiven and changed by God's love.

As you come into the Cathedral, pause to remember your own vulnerable humanity, the hopes and fears and burdens that you bring with you as you enter. And give thanks too for the love of God which has drawn you here, as it has drawn so many people over the ages.

✠

Prayer

Almighty God, in Christ you make all things new:
transform the poverty of our nature
by the riches of your grace,
and in the renewal of our lives
make known your heavenly glory.

Alternative Service Book 1980

The Nave

The Nave

Now go into the Cathedral itself and stand at the back by the west door. Look up at the roof and appreciate its 300 feet of unbroken length and its height of 66 feet. Look at the pillars and lift your eyes to the vaulting of the roof. The whole has the appearance of an avenue of giant palms, sculpted in warm stone. The fan vaulting is peculiar to Exeter among the cathedrals of England. The fans are keyed together by bosses. You can use a mirror trolley to see them, without having to crane your neck. The martyrdom of Thomas à Beckett is depicted above you, too high for the commissioners of Henry VIII to destroy, as he wished. It is a reminder of the futility of human attempts to rewrite reality, and the enduring witness of faith.

Meditation

The church is the perfect image of the
sensible world.
For sky it has the divine sanctuary,
and for earth the nave in all its beauty.
And vice versa the world is a church.

For sanctuary it has sky
and for nave the grandeur of the earth.

Maximus the Confessor

To your right you will see the flag (encased) that was given to Captain Scott by Queen Alexandra and used as a sledge flag on his first expedition to the South Pole. To your left is the Chapel of St Edmund, the chapel of the Devonshire Regiment, containing memorials to those men of Devon who left home never to return.

The Nave Pulpit

The pulpit is a memorial to a great Devon missionary – John Coleridge Patteson, the first Bishop of Melanesia. When he was a boy at Eton, George Selwyn, the Bishop of New Zealand, preached in the chapel, and Patteson heard the call to be a missionary – a calling from which he never swerved. He was murdered by native islanders at Nakapu in 1871. The central panel of the pulpit shows his martyrdom. The left-hand panel shows the death of St Alban, the first British martyr. To the right is St Boniface, another martyr from Devon. So it is that in the beauty and peace of this Cathedral we are reminded of the passion, agony and sacrifice of those who followed the example of Jesus, and those who suffer today for their faithfulness as his disciples.

Prayer

We thank thee, O Lord, for all who have chosen
poverty or solitude for thy sake,
for men and women of prayer,
for saints in common life
who have borne suffering for noble ends,
and for those who have endured pain
with patience and purity of life,
in the strength of him who,
for the joy that was set before him,
endured the cross,
even Jesus Christ our Lord.

The Corbels

On the pillar beyond the pulpit you will see one of the many corbels which decorate this building. A corbel is a bracket-like block of stone which projects from the face of the wall to support the vaulting shaft above. This particular corbel represents an acrobat performing above a fiddler playing. It was carved by Roger, who died in 1310; a dog (at the foot) is the mark of his work. The scene may well have had its origin in the ancient French tale known as 'Our Lady's Tumbler' which tells how a fairground acrobat entered a monastery, and, ashamed to find that he had no great gift or talent to offer God, secretly took to performing acrobatics in front of the

statue of the Virgin. He simply offered what he was able to give.

On the opposite pillar there is the figure of the Blessed Virgin and the Holy Child, mutilated by the bullets of Cromwell's soldiers in the seventeenth century. The bullet-marks remind us of the all-too-human capacity of one group of Christians to reject and ridicule the religious aspirations of another.

Prayer

God, who art the God of peace,
mercifully grant that, as much lieth in us,
we may live at peace with all;
and if our outward peace be broken,
yet do thou preserve peace in our hearts;
through him who is the Prince of Peace,
Jesus Christ our Lord.

✠

The Minstrels' Gallery

High on the north wall you will see the front of a gallery which masks a large room behind. It is decorated with fourteen angels playing medieval instruments. It is from here that the choir sing carols at

Christmas-time. When the gallery was built in the fourteenth century, the Cathedral had fourteen boy choristers, and was as well supplied as any cathedral in England with the treble line. The sound of treble voices floating from a high place would tempt the eye to look upwards to the fourteen musical angels on the gallery front, and because the choristers could not be seen it seemed that the ethereal sound came from the angels themselves. The Minstrels' Gallery, one of the few in existence, depicts the angels playing upon the following instruments: citole, bagpipes, recorder, viol, harp, Jew's harp, trumpet, organ, gittern, shawm, timbrel and cymbals. There are a number of singing galleries inside and outside the Cathedral, which were designed to enliven services of worship by the element of surprise and to enrich the liturgy by a variety of sound and movement. This enabled people to appreciate that the worship of the Church on earth joined with the music of heaven.

✠

Meditation

O may we soon again renew that Song,
and keep in tune with Heaven, 'til God 'ere long
To his celestial consort us unite,
To live with Him, and sing in endless morn of light.

John Milton

The organ and the Pulpitum

The Organ and the Pulpitum

The Organ

As you stand in the Nave and look east, the organ with its delightfully glorious case occupies a dominant position. In common with other cathedrals, there was a tradition from the Middle Ages of placing the organ on the Quire screen. It was not universally popular, and many organs have been removed from that lofty setting. Many pilgrims find the organ's position obtrusive and feel that it interrupts the view to the East Window. Others feel strongly that it is rightly placed, because it can in that position serve both Quire and Nave with its magnificent sound. More than that, it provides a sense of mystery by partially hiding the beauty of the Quire and the High Altar beyond. John Betjeman, the poet, thought that 'The screen organ case stops the building from becoming a long vaulted tunnel.' In the tradition of Eastern Christians, the most holy part of the building is always hidden from view behind the screen.

The organ has in its time suffered from unpopularity. During the Cromwellian period the larger part of the organ was destroyed and its pipes were carried through the streets of Exeter by Cromwell's soldiers. The present case, with certain alterations, was put here thirty years before Bach was born. Music in worship has a long pedigree. It also arouses strong feelings, and the necessary tension between old and new music is one that keeps music alive and relevant. The aim is to provide the best that we can offer. Music's fundamental purpose is to give glory to God, to foster and deepen the fellowship of those who sing together, and to create the mood of worship which an organ can do so well – sometimes gentle and quiet, sometimes strong and affirming, and at Easter, Christmas and Pentecost powerful in celebration and praise.

Prayer

Almighty God,
you have ordained that the hearts of men and women
shall be kindled by music,
and their minds thereby attuned
to understand your divine mysteries.
Teach us to love you in all your gifts
and to trace your hand in all your works,
so that we may join the music of our worship here
with the music of heaven.

The Pulpitum

The organ case stands on the screen which is called the 'Pulpitum' in the old fabric accounts. The Pulpitum divides the Nave from the Quire. The Nave is the public part of the Cathedral where people learn and listen and pray, and where processions regularly take place. Here any of the business of a church may be conducted. It is a symbol of the world in which we live. Within the screen is a world only half seen, dim and distant enough to prevent any clear-cut vision, though we can recognize that there is something there. This symbolizes the world to come, into which we dare enter only through the merits of Christ.

The Pulpitum has two altars in front of it – those of St Mary and St Nicholas. St Mary's altar on the left is often called 'Brattan's altar' because in front of it was buried Henry de Brattan, one of the greatest of English lawyers and Chancellor of the Cathedral in the time of Bishop Bronescombe.

The Pulpitum forms a dramatic barrier between the Nave and the Quire. During acts of worship in medieval times it formed an elevated platform for the singing of the Gospels. The frieze of paintings on the Pulpitum screen, painted in the early seventeenth century, provides a sumptuous entrance to the Quire from the Nave.

Move to the north (left-hand) end of the Pulpitum and prayerfully follow the sequence of paintings round, as they represent these scenes from the Old and New Testaments: the Creation; Eve originating from Adam's side; the Flood; Pharaoh's host overwhelmed in the Red Sea; the destruction of Solomon's Temple; the building of the Second Temple; the angel's appearance to Zacharias; the nativity of Jesus; his baptism; his being taken down from the Cross; the Resurrection; the Ascension; the descent of the Holy Spirit at Pentecost. As you look, you trace in your pilgrimage the story of God's action in history and the story of our redemption in Christ. Here is a pilgrim's prayer:

Prayer

Give me my scallop-shell of quiet,
My staff of faith to walk upon,
My scrip of joy, immortal diet,
My bottle of salvation;
My gown of glory (hope's true gauge),
And thus I'll take my pilgrimage.

Sir Walter Raleigh

✠

The South Transept

This is the busiest place in the Cathedral. Visitors come here looking for the shop and for stewards and guides; and others, who have finished their visit, go from here in search of the Chapter House and the Refectory. Just like the space under the tower on the other side of the Cathedral, the South Transept is a storage area. Here are a piano, a model of the Cathedral for the blind, and other pieces of furniture. More substantial things are also here, including the magnificent tomb of the Second Earl of Devon and his wife. Originally they lay in the Nave, and were moved here many years ago to be out of the way. And against the west wall are the vast organ pipes which make some of the deepest notes of all (though not the loudest), stretching up to the roof. On the same wall is the operating board for the Cathedral's lighting.

Here is one of the 'off-stage' places of the Cathedral, where choristers can be found lining up before they go to the vestry, or where orchestral players get ready for a performance. It's a place of preparation.

Stained glass in the Chapel of St John the Baptist

The Chapel of St John the Baptist

Suitably enough, the chapel on the east side of the South Transept is dedicated to St John the Baptist. He is a good patron saint for people getting ready for any great event. The cousin of Jesus, he is called 'the Forerunner', because he preached that someone greater than he – the Messiah – would shortly come to cleanse and renew the people of God. A copy of a painting by Leonardo da Vinci hangs near the chapel. It depicts Jesus and John as children, playing at the side of their mothers, St Mary and her sister St Elizabeth.

The chapel itself is surprisingly serene. There is little carving or decoration, but the light through the south window often falls brilliantly on the golden stone. This chapel is used for robing before and after services, and sometimes confessions are heard here. It is an ideal place to draw aside and get ready. In the window is a scene of St John baptizing Jesus in the river Jordan, with other scenes of St John's life all around.

✠

Meditation

You will go before the Lord to prepare his way,
to give light to those who sit in darkness
and the shadow of death,
and to guide our feet into the way of peace.

Luke 1:76,79

The Bells

High above the South Transept hang the bells of the Cathedral. Bells are the oldest music of the Church. The belfry is as much a distinguishing mark for Western Christian churches as the minaret is for the mosque. During the late Middle Ages the English developed the tradition of swinging their bells through a whole circle on a wheel. A few rings of bells survive from before the Reformation, but the craze for ringing reached its height in the seventeenth century. The ringers have developed elaborate patterns by which they haul on their bellropes, and this makes one of the most English of sounds.

Although enthusiastic ringers have taken the tradition to other places around the world, this country is the heart of the practice.

Exeter has fourteen bells which can be swung in the South Tower, and which make the second heaviest ring in the world – a challenge to any team of bell-ringers! On the great festivals of the Church's year, they are rung at 6 a.m. and can be heard for many miles. They have historic and strange names such as Stafford, Grandisson, Earle, Pennington and Pongamouth.

Every day one of the bells, 'Little Nine o'Clock', is rung for services, as it was centuries ago before the main Mass of the day. The newest bell is 'Jubilee', cast to celebrate the Silver Jubilee of Queen Elizabeth II in 1977. The bells of Exeter are an uninterrupted tradition, proclaiming to the world that the Cathedral is at prayer, and they are a sign of God's presence to those who hear and cannot come.

✠

Prayer

O God,
grant that those who shall be called
by the ringing of these bells to worship you
may enter your gates with thanksgiving
and come into your courts with praise.

The Chapter House

If you have the time and it is open, you may like to visit the Chapter House. Go through the door by the organ pipes and straight ahead down the steps. It was built in the early 1200s and was rebuilt with a high roof after a fire in the fifteenth century. There is an intriguing set of modern fibreglass-and-aluminium sculptures in the arcades, created by Kenneth Carter in 1974. They depict moments in the Creation and events from the life of Christ. The powerful mixture of old and new is a metaphor of the ongoing vitality of the Church's faith, with each generation building on what has gone before.

✠

Meditation

Every scribe who has been trained
for the kingdom of heaven
is like the host who brings out of his treasure
what is new and what is old.

Matthew 13:52

The North Transept

The Clock

Now walk back over the crossing to the base of the North Tower by the clock. Any visit to an ancient building reminds us of the transient nature of life itself. Facing the clock, we are reminded of this even more forcefully. We stand in a tower built in the early twelfth century by the grandchildren of the Normans and Saxons who fought over who would rule England. Their dynasties are long gone. There was a clock here by the end of the thirteenth century, marking out the hours of the thirty generations that have passed since then.

The present clock is thought to have been the gift of Bishop Peter Courtenay at the end of the fifteenth century, and puts the earth at the centre. Around it revolve the moon in its phases and the fleur-de-lis of the sun, which tells both the hours and the lunar day. The upper dial showing the minutes was added in the eighteenth century. The clock rings the sole bell in the North Tower on the hours.

Called 'Great Peter', it was also the Bishop's gift. Weighing four tons, it is the oldest bell of its weight in Britain.

Over the centuries countless thousands have stood here and seen not only the time, but also the message which the clock conveys: *Pereunt et imputantur* – that is, 'They [the hours] perish and are reckoned to our account.' Time passes, and we also will have our account to give. Those who had put the earth at the centre of the universe have already learned better. We as pilgrims today may know much more about the cosmos, but we know no more than our predecessors did about our eternal destiny. Pilgrimage is a time to make sure that we know what – or who – is at the centre of our own lives. As 'Great Peter' tolls out the hours, we may recall these famous words of John Donne, Dean of St Paul's in London, about the custom of ringing the bell for a funeral:

Meditation

Who bends not his ear to any bell
which upon any occasion rings?
But who can remove it from that bell
which is passing a piece of himself out of this world?
No man is an island, entire of itself;
every man is a piece of the continent, a part of the main.
If a clod be washed away by the sea,
Europe is the less,

as well as if a promontory were,
as well as if a manor of thy friend's or of thine own were:
any man's death diminishes me,
because I am involved in mankind.
And therefore never send to know
for whom the bell tolls;
it tolls for thee.

John Donne

The Chapels

The chapel on the right is dedicated to St Paul, the great saint who spread the gospel into the Greek world. The carpet and kneelers bear words from his letters, the very lively correspondence which kept the early Christians in touch with each other. The chapel contains an icon of St Peter and St Paul given by Exeter's partnership diocese of Cyprus and the Gulf.

The other chapel is the chantry chapel in the corner, built by Precentor Sylke in the early 1500s out of the former Chapel of the Cross. It shows two of the preoccupations of late medieval religion. One is the concern with the reality of physical death. So there is the very dead (and now legless) effigy with its Latin inscription which means: 'As I am so you will be.' In this corner of the Cathedral we are not allowed to forget our mortality. Looking through the memorial on to the north wall of the chapel, you will see a reconstruction of the original wall painting which shows the burial of Christ. 'As I am so you will be' – dead and buried!

But there was more to Sylke's religion than despair. The chantry was set up for an annuellar (a priest saying regular Masses), so that the living might pray for the salvation of their dead. Now look up – over the chapel is a painting of the resurrection of Christ. Time passes, and 'as I am' so shall we all be – dead and buried, but risen with Christ. We journey through time in the company of the saints, and with our prayers we strengthen one another in the face of the power of death, which Christ has overcome.

✠

Meditation

Let nothing disturb you;
let nothing frighten you;
all thing pass;
God never changes.
Patience achieves
all that it strives for.
If we have God
we find we lack nothing.
God only meets all our needs.

St Teresa of Avila

The North Quire Aisle

St Anne teaching the Virgin to read

As you move away from the North Transept, turn left into the North Quire Aisle. This is the beginning of the Ambulatory, the passageway built for processions around the Cathedral's central worship space in the Quire. It has something of the feeling of an in-between space: the roof is more functional, the space is filled with monuments and displays rather than important features. This is a passage which is going somewhere.

In our lives we may have times when we feel like we're travelling rather than arriving, and yet there is much to see and learn on the way. That is also the case here in this passage. On the right, backing onto the Quire, are items of history and information, illustrating something of the richness of the Cathedral's life. On the left are some of the many memorials to those who have died. Here is further witness to the communion of the saints, the people who have run their course of life, and yet look on us as we follow ours. Think about the inscriptions, especially the sadness of lives cut short by accident or war. Human tragedy and human hope are inseparably bound together.

The Chapel of St Andrew and St Catherine

Halfway down the aisle on the left is the chapel dedicated to St Andrew and St Catherine. St Andrew's altar has behind it a modern window by Sir Ninian Comper in memory of those who survived the sinking of HMS *Exeter* during the Second World War. A young-looking Jesus calls a sinking Peter back up from the water on which he walks – a reminder that, without the help of Christ, none of us can survive the deep waters of death. The stone canopy against the far wall may once have graced a tomb. In the corner of the chapel is a door which gives the choir and organist access to the Song School, where they keep and rehearse music in a room which was originally the Cathedral's treasury.

The chapel is now used as a place to remember aspects of 'Justice, Peace and the Integrity of Creation', which the World Council of Churches has encouraged its member churches to do. Environmental damage, social need, poverty and injustice are marked here by temporary exhibitions, and you are invited to respond in prayer and other ways. The

Cathedral, like all churches, is not a place of refuge away from the world, but is a place where the world's sorrows are seen in their proper perspective in relation to the God of love and justice. The saints who witness our pilgrimage through life will also make their judgements about the particular ways in which we fail to honour God's life in others and in the world of our own day.

✠

Prayers

O Lord,
baptize our hearts into a sense
of the needs and conditions of all.

George Fox

God, who created us in your own image,
grant us grace fearlessly to contend against evil
and to make no peace with oppression;
and, that we may reverently use our freedom,
help us to employ it in the maintenance of justice
in our communities and among the nations.

American Prayer Book 1979

The Tombs

Going left out of the chapel, you will see on your left a cadaver tomb of the sort that was fashionable in the sixteenth century, the most death-like in this Cathedral. As with Sylke's Chantry, you don't need to read Latin to get the message: 'Look at what you will become, and turn to Christ.'

There are three interesting tombs of former bishops on the inner wall of the North Quire Aisle. Bishops liked to be buried near the High Altar, as a sign of wanting to be close to Christ. First is the tomb of Henry Marshall (bishop 1194–1206), moved here when the new Cathedral was built, and beautifully carved in his likeness. The second tomb is now plain and unmarked, due to the actions of Henry VIII's reforming Dean Simon Heynes. Edmund Lacy was a holy man who died in 1455, and whose tomb became a place for people to ask for his help after he had died, just as they had when he lived. The tomb was once festooned with wax models of arms, legs and other body parts which needed healing. A cache of them was found above the tomb in 1943.

The final and most splendid tomb is that of Bishop Walter Stapledon, who was murdered by the London mob in 1326 while trying to govern the city on behalf of the unpopular King Edward II. The figure lies in state, apparently restful. But if you look closely through the grating at the inner ceiling of the tomb, you can see the painted figure of Christ showing his five wounds. Even in death, the great bishop has to look to the sufferings of Jesus in order to find salvation: it's not Stapledon's robes or reputation which will help him now, but his trust in his Saviour.

*

Meditation

It is Christ Jesus who died,
yes, who was raised,
who is at the right hand of God
and intercedes for us.
So who will separate us from the love of Christ?
Neither death, nor life, nor angels, nor rulers,
nor things present, nor things to come,
nor anything else in all creation,
will be able to separate us from the love of God
in Christ Jesus our Lord.

Romans 8:34

The Lady Chapel

In English cathedrals, the easternmost part of the building is often dedicated to Mary, the mother of Jesus, and is called the 'Chapel of our Lady' or simply the 'Lady Chapel'. At Exeter, this is one of the most beautiful parts of the whole Cathedral. Coming across it after passing the grandeur of the Quire feels like reaching a destination. It is kept as a quiet place, where visitors often leave prayers and light candles.

A statue of Mary stands on the south side under an arch. In her arms she holds Jesus, shown as a little child. He in turn opens his arms towards us, as if delighted to see us and welcoming us. Mary's whole purpose is to bring us to pay attention to Christ. Sometimes she is called the 'star of the sea', the one who guides us across the waters of life as reliably as the Pole Star. When Jesus was beginning his ministry he attended a wedding at Cana (John 2:1–12). When the wine ran out, Mary was asked what to do. She directed them to Jesus with the words: 'Do whatever he tells you.' This is always Mary's message.

But many Christians feel special tenderness to Mary for her own sake. She was the perfect partner in the birth of Jesus, and in being born from her Jesus inherited all the characteristics – physical and mental

– which made him a human being. There is no better way of praying than doing as Mary would often have done: just gazing at and enjoying the One she bore.

Prayer

O Christ our God incarnate,
whose Virgin mother was blessed in bearing you,
but still more blessed in keeping your word;
grant us, who honour the exaltation of her lowliness,
to follow the example of her devotion to your will.

William Bright

The east window portrays many scenes from the life of Christ. In the centre, Mary is shown holding her son, who receives the adoration of the shepherds and wise men. But heaven and earth, stars and angels, are all present in the scene, showing that the birth of Christ is the most important moment since the creation of the universe.

The striking needlework on the altar frontal, executed by the Royal School of Needlework, shows a flourishing oak tree in the circle. The idea comes from the design of oak leaves along the screen behind the altar. But here the tree stands for all that God has made on earth, which receives God's love continually.

The Lady Chapel is full of lovely details, such as the shepherds carved in wood on the west wall. This scene is taken from the story of Christ's birth. This fifteenth-century carving is a tenderly and skilfully made sculpture, and conveys a sense of happiness and peace.

The Tombs

Some fine tombs of different periods are placed around the walls, including the ancient stone under the statue of Mary. This is said to be the tomb of Bishop Leofric, the founder of the Cathedral before the Norman Conquest. But the stone is of a later date and was moved here long after his lifetime.

Two more magnificent tombs to great bishops are on either side as you enter the Lady Chapel. The one on the right is that of Bishop Walter Bronescombe, one of the builders of the Cathedral. This was carved from basalt after he died in 1280, but has kept much of its colour. The whole statue of the bishop is delicately carved and full of vitality. His eyes are open, and he is dressed in the gorgeous robes of a bishop of the time. Such a tomb has no trace of lamentation about it. Bronescombe was a bishop in an age when the magnificence of the Church was accepted as a sign of divine power, and a bishop was seen as a sign of God's presence and blessing.

Even the highly coloured seventeenth-century tomb of Lady Dodderidge on the north wall carries the sense of hopefulness. She lies in her fashionable dress as if merely resting. A quaint poem underneath in Latin and English speaks of death as a clock being taken to pieces and reassembled. All through the Lady Chapel runs the theme of God's life-giving power. He gave life through the creation of all things, in the birth of Christ, and in the power to overcome death.

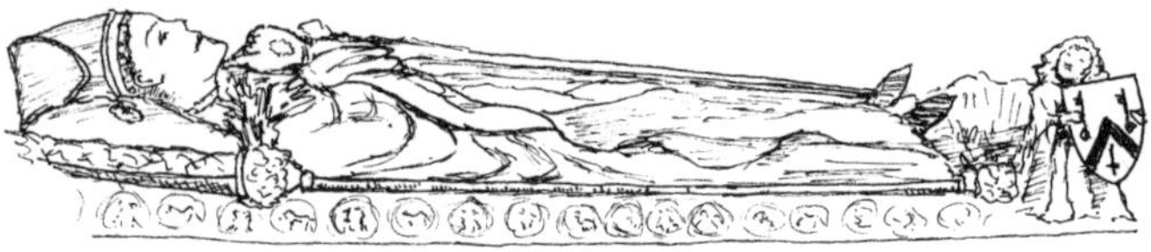

The tomb of Bishop Bronescombe in the Lady Chapel

Prayer

You in whom all things live,
you command us to seek you,
and are ever ready to be found.
To know you is life, to serve you is freedom,
to praise you is our souls' joy.
We bless and adore you, we worship and exalt you,
we praise you for your great glory.

St Augustine

The South Quire Aisle

As you turn left out of the Lady Chapel, you enter the South Quire Aisle. The south-east corner of the Cathedral is the part which has been least touched by time and change. The screen of the Chapel of St Gabriel keeps much of its ancient colour, with red and gold paint disguising the stonework. On the old wooden doors (still with their original fastenings) there is a charming painting of the angel Gabriel appearing to Mary, as described in Luke's Gospel. This is the beginning of the life of Jesus, and the words of Gabriel, 'Hail, Mary, full of grace!' set the scene for the coming of Christ and the age of grace.

'Angel' means 'messenger', and the angels are to be thought of as the heavenly beings who bring to us the power and encouragement of God. If we can imagine heaven at all, we should imagine it full of life, full of living beings who transmit God's will into action in heaven and on earth. Churches have traditionally been carved with many angels. They have a generally human form, because the human form is the 'image and likeness of God'. But they have wings (of a kind which are simply decorative) to show that they do not belong to this world.

The coming of the Reformation meant that nearly

all the pictures and statues of angels and of saints which once filled the walls of churches were taken away or covered up. As a result it is hard to imagine how colourfully decorated the churches once were. But it is very likely that many of the pictures would have disappeared anyway as fashions changed. The irony is that the whitewash that was put over them has sometimes helped to preserve them.

Prayer

Therefore with angels and archangels,
and with all the company of heaven,
we proclaim your great and glorious name.

Alternative Service Book 1980

The Coronation of the Virgin

A few years ago the painting of Mary high on the wall to the left of the Chapel of St Gabriel was uncovered. It was painted not long before the Reformation, and was probably part of a large portrayal of the death of Mary and her coronation in heaven. The lower part has been covered by a later memorial. What we can still see is Mary surrounded by a glorious cloud of light, being welcomed into heaven by the angels. The Church Fathers long ago decided, from careful reading of the Bible, that there are nine different kinds of angels, and here they all are: thrones, dominations,

The coronation of the Virgin (left) and the Chapel of St Gabriel (right)

principalities, powers, cherubs, seraphs and the rest. They even have little labels to make it clear who is who. At the top God the Father and Jesus lean out, waiting to give Mary a crown.

Many Christians, both when this painting was made and now, make a special place in their prayers for Mary, the mother of the Lord. Her willingness to let God use her to fulfil his purposes makes Mary an excellent example of humble love. So prayers linked to Mary are tender and intimate. She shows us the sort of people we can be if we allow the love of God to fill our lives. The coronation of Mary, shown in this old painting, is meant to be a promise for us as well. In giving Mary a crown of life in heaven, God shows what he intends for all who have faith throughout their lives: 'Be faithful until death, and I will give you the crown of life' (Revelation 1:11).

The Chapel of St Gabriel

Inside the Chapel of St Gabriel is the cupboard in which are kept the bread and wine from the Holy Communion. A light burns continually outside. This consecrated food is taken to those who are sick and unable to come to church. This is, quite naturally, a quiet and holy place, where people can sit and pray without interruption. Above the ancient stone altar is a very simple metal crucifix. The human form of Jesus in his suffering is reduced to basic shapes. It is as if he leans forward towards us, and the one coloured detail is what is nearest to us, as if he holds out to us his love and forgiveness even as he dies.

There is another portrayal of Jesus in the window above. This window was assembled from pieces of ancient glass, and the central panel is taken from a picture of Jesus on the Cross. All that is left is his head and body, but they have been arranged so that he seems now to look down in tenderness and suffering towards the light which marks the reserved bread and wine.

The Chapel of St Gabriel draws us to spend time in quiet in the presence of the son of Mary, who has promised to be with us 'to the end of the age' (Matthew 28:20). What Christ gained for us cost him pain and death, but he did it all willingly, for love of us.

✠

Prayer

We thank you
because by the power of your Holy Spirit
your Son Jesus took our nature upon him
when he was born of the Virgin Mary his mother,
that being himself without sin,
he might make us clean from all sin.

Alternative Service Book 1980

The Oldham Chapel

Next to the Chapel of St Gabriel is the richly carved Chapel of St Saviour and St Boniface. This was built by Bishop Hugh Oldham as his burial place and chantry, where prayers could be offered for his soul. It was built to match Sir John Speke's chantry in the North Quire Aisle, which also has beautiful carved work including a small gem depicting the Virgin Mary's mother teaching her to read. The coloured effigy of Bishop Oldham, who died in 1519, lies in the south wall of his chapel. It is said that he was too modest to be buried in the Cathedral, and so his body was placed in a bulge of the wall, so as to be (strictly speaking) outside it. For all that, Oldham's chantry was carved splendidly. Though some of the carvings have been destroyed, we can still find Oldham's 'owls' (his emblem, punning on his name) strutting about in the stonework.

An owl carving from the Oldham Chapel

Oldham was a famous bishop. In his time there was a great advance in education, and many schools and colleges were being founded to meet the demand to train men in the law. Oldham is still commemorated every year by the pupils of Manchester Grammar School, which he founded.

The Church has always felt a deep responsibility for education. Many of our schools were begun by the Church, and to this day there are great numbers of Church schools throughout the country. 'Godliness and good learning' have often been cultivated together.

✠

Prayer

Heavenly Father, with whom are hid
the treasures of wisdom and knowledge:
in your mercy save your children from misusing
these your gifts for selfish and destructive ends,
that they may be used only for your glory
and the common good.

Church of Scotland

Damage and Renewal

In May 1942 Exeter was devastated by bombs. Half of the ancient city was flattened or burnt out. Many lovely buildings were lost, and the scars remain. Perhaps it was intended that the Cathedral should be spared, and it was a great relief to the people of Devon that after the raids were over, the towers and roofs of the Cathedral still stood among the ruins.

But the Cathedral was hit. One high-explosive bomb landed on the chapel to the south of the Quire. Had it landed a few feet further north, the damage would have been far greater; had it landed a few yards to the south, the Bishop's Palace would have been lost. As it was, the damage was serious enough. It left a gaping hole, and inside the Cathedral the monuments and screens were shattered. You can see in the doorway of the screen how the pieces were assembled. People call it 'the biggest jigsaw puzzle in the world'. Up and down the South Quire Aisle the cracks in the monuments show how they have been skilfully put together again.

The Chapel of St James and St Thomas

At the entrance of the chapel on a plinth stands a small statue of a shepherd reaching out to help one of his flock. Crafted by the American sculptor Roseanne Keller in 1995, it represents a vision of Jesus that she had while walking on Hatterall Ridge.

The Chapel of St James and St Thomas was rebuilt as it was before the bombing, with the addition of a few interesting corbels (look for the cat and mouse!). An inscription on the wall gives thanks for the restoration of the Cathedral. A special service was held fifty years after the raid, and it was attended by the German ambassador. The chapel now stands as a sign of reconciliation in the wake of the conflict. In this chapel also hang standards of the Devon and Dorset Regiment, with their roll of honour. Here we remember those who died in the cause of peace, for which we continue to pray.

A cat corbel from St James' Chapel

Prayer

O Lord God, when thou givest to thy servants
to endeavour any great matter,
grant us also to know that it is not the beginning
but the continuing of the same until the end,
until it be thoroughly finished,
which yieldeth the true glory;
through him who for the finishing of thy work
laid down his life,
our Redeemer Jesus Christ.

Sir Francis Drake

✠

The Bishops

Opposite the St James Chapel is the back of the Bishop's throne, a wonder of ancient woodwork. Fortunately this was taken down during the War and stored. Had it stayed, it would have been completely destroyed.

The Bishops of Exeter are commemorated in this part of the Cathedral by several tombs and memorials. A cathedral is primarily the seat (or *cathedra*) of a bishop, and is the focus for his leadership and his care of his diocese. The Bishops, whose estates and wealth financed much of this building, intended that it should be a dazzling sign of God's presence in this part of England. Until 1877, their diocese ran from the county border with Dorset and Somerset to the Isles of Scilly.

You will find among these memorials a fine one to Bishop Weston (died 1742). Before he was a Bishop he had been a schoolmaster, and the Latin inscription seems to have been just finished by a graceful angel. Another memorial is to Bishop Cotton (died 1626). It is decorated with a cherub blowing bubbles, to remind us how fragile life is. His grandson, Edward Cotton (died 1675), was a Canon Treasurer here, and is portrayed in a bust which shows a highly intelligent and refined face.

Here is a place to pray for the mission of the Church in Devon today. Please pray for the Bishop of Exeter; for the suffragan Bishops of Crediton and

Plymouth; for the parishes and those who minister in them; for all the people of the Church, lay and ordained, who share Christ's ministry in our part of the world.

Prayer

O God, most glorious, most bountiful,
accept we humbly pray our praises and thanksgivings
for your holy Church Universal,
the Mother of us all who bear the name of Christ:
for the faith which it has conveyed in safety to our time,
and the mercies by which it has enlarged and comforted
the souls of men and women;
for the virtues which it has established upon earth,
and the holy lives by which it glorifies
both the world and you.

Lancelot Andrewes

✠

The Quire

Move from the South Quire Aisle by the Bishop's throne into the middle of the Quire, and look west towards the organ. Here in the centre of the Cathedral is the place where the choir sing the daily office. Worship and music are the most essential part of the Cathedral's life. The special quality of English cathedral music has a unique ability to uplift the soul. Cromwell removed the organs and music from the Cathedral – he thought music was too exciting for religion! After King Charles II came back to England in 1660 the organ case was restored.

The Choir Stalls

Prayers have been said in this building every day since it was built. The Quire was the place where traditionally the Cathedral 'family' met for its daily prayers. The Dean and the Precentor sat underneath the organ, the Chancellor next to the Bishop's throne, and the Treasurer opposite the throne – in the four corners of the Quire, as it were. The stalls that you see today were made during Gilbert Scott's restoration in the 1870s, in Decorated style to match the character of the building. Scott retained the medieval seating arrangement (separate tiers for canons, vicars and clerks), together with the original misericords (tip-up half-seats for leaning on while standing) and their lively carvings, including the famous elephant on display in the South Quire Aisle. The choir now sings from the centre stalls with the red lamps. The Cathedral's choir consists of up to twenty boy and twenty girl choristers, with fourteen lay vicars and choral scholars. When the choir is on holiday, services may be sung by visiting groups or by the Cathedral's own voluntary choir. Together with the organists, the choir form a dedicated group whose skill and commitment are put at the service of singing God's praises.

The Bishop's Throne

The throne is at the end of the stalls. Fifty-seven feet high, it was carved in a few years after 1312, and shows tremendous skill in its workmanship. The figures of the bishops at its base were repainted by Scott. The statue of St Peter near the top, carved by

The Bishop's throne

Herbert Read, was modelled on Bishop William Cecil (died 1935). The throne was made to emphasize the importance of the Bishops of Exeter, but it was placed in the Quire as a reminder that their authority was ultimately spiritual and was based on prayer and worship.

This whole building is founded on prayer. Pause and thank God for the privilege of prayer, and bring to him your own prayers, remembering the countless others who, through hundreds of years, have prayed in this place.

✠

Prayer

May the strength of God pilot us.
May the power of God preserve us.
May the wisdom of God instruct us.
May the hand of God protect us.
May the way of God direct us.
May the shield of God defend us.
May the host of God guard us.
May Christ be with us, Christ before us,
Christ in us, Christ over us.
May your salvation, O Lord,
be always ours this day and for ever.

St Patrick's Breastplate

The High Altar

As you turn in the middle of the Quire to face east, you see the space which lies at the heart of the Cathedral, the place where the Holy Table is set and the Eucharist or Holy Communion is celebrated. Just as in medieval times, the Eucharist is also often celebrated today elsewhere in the Cathedral – at the Nave altar or in the side chapels – but the High Altar is the architectural climax of the Cathedral and symbolizes the joining of earth and heaven. The steps in the magnificent floor installed in Sir Gilbert Scott's remodelling of the Quire emphasize the sense of focus, with the Holy Table on the highest step. The higher part of the Quire is called the Presbytery, which means 'the priests' place'. It has something of the old Jewish Temple's 'Holy of Holies' about it.

The Table itself is unremarkable – wooden, it dates from the Victorian period. It is made to be covered. The altar frontal is changed to reflect the season and mood of the celebration: green for ordinary times; white or gold for Christmas and Easter, the times of rejoicing; purple or blue for sad and penitential times, in Advent and Lent; red for the Holy Spirit and the inspired martyrs – notably St Peter, to whom the Cathedral is dedicated. The flowers which may be set in the sanctuary also reflect something of the season. The Christian faith is not only believed or imagined, but is expressed through the material things which God himself has created.

On the right-hand side of the Presbytery you can see the medieval sedilia, the seats where the celebrant sat flanked by his deacon and sub-deacon during part of the service. This magnificently ornate seating was badly damaged by the bombing in 1942, and was expertly restored by Herbert Read.

The Exeter Pillar

Behind the Table you can see the Exeter Pillar. Up until 1939 this was obscured by a large reredos (a backdrop to the High Altar covered in statues, of the kind which can be seen in many cathedrals and churches today) and was only visible from the Ambulatory by the Lady Chapel. Altogether the Cathedral has had four reredoses. The last one, Scott's, was given to Heavitree Parish Church, due to structural problems and changes in taste.

The style of the Exeter Pillar is very important. As the Cathedral was being built westwards, the patterns of the pillars varied slightly, as you can see at the corners of the Presbytery and at the entrance to the Lady Chapel. This lozenge-shaped central pillar was made with four columns of unpolished Purbeck marble on each side, and it gave its form to both lines of pillars marching down the rest of the Cathedral. This is the only central pillar in the building, and it holds up the east wall and the East Window. We speak sometimes of saints, living or dead, as 'pillars of the Church': here is a living metaphor of their faith and dedication.

*

Meditation

Come to him, a living stone,
chosen and precious in God's sight,
and like living stones
let yourselves be built into a spiritual house,
to be a holy priesthood,
to offer spiritual sacrifices acceptable to God
through Jesus Christ.

1 Peter 2:5

The Great East Window

As you look up at the magnificent East Window, you are reminded that you are in the company of the saints – not to mention all those myriad people who, over the last 800 or so years, have stood near this spot as pilgrims, and have prayed here and have looked at the pictures of the saints who have gone before them.

The window was glazed in 1304. Because its stonework became unsafe, it was re-glazed in 1391 in the new Perpendicular style (see how the vertical columns of the frame go all the way to the top, unlike the other Cathedral windows). It has been substantially reworked at intervals since then.

The top three lights are from the original window: on the left is Abraham looking up, then Moses, and then Isaiah – three precursors to Christ. Abraham was himself a pilgrim, setting off he knew not where, and he leads us on.

There are two local saints in the next row: St Sidwell, with her sickle, and St Helena, the mother of Constantine. She allegedly found a part of the True Cross, which she stands holding. She went as a pilgrim to the Holy Land looking for relics – things that would put her in touch with the living Jesus. In a similar way, many people come into this Cathedral in order to be close to Christ.

In the middle of the window are two archangels and an oddly placed St Catherine. To her right is King Edward the Confessor, who was one of the founders of this Cathedral. He stood near where you are now to make Leofric the first Bishop of Exeter in the eleventh century. Next to him is the martyr Edmund, holding the arrows with which he was killed. So we offer to God the sufferings inflicted on us.

In the bottom left-hand corner of the window is St Margaret of Antioch, sometimes called Marina. Her story was thought to be apocryphal as early as the fifth century and consists of a series of fantastic escapades. In one she was swallowed by a dragon, representing Satan, but the crucifix she carried so irritated his throat that he spewed her out. The legend has persisted, because it reminds us that whatever dragons of despair or difficulty we face, the Cross can lead us to an answer.

Next to St Margaret is another depiction of St Catherine, holding the wheel on which she was broken. The upper figure of Catherine is offside, because all the saints on the right-hand side of the window are men and all the ones on the left are women. At some stage glass from elsewhere was re-used in this window, resulting in the duplication of St Catherine!

Third on the bottom row is Mary Magdalene with her jar of ointment. Tradition says that she poured rich ointment over Jesus, representing the offering of the very best of the earth. This Cathedral, with all its excellence and the cost in human terms of its building, is an example of the very best that we can offer to God, who is above all; and it is an invitation to us to offer all that we have in response to God's love for us.

In the centre of the bottom row is the Madonna and Child – Mary holding the baby Jesus. He is the central figure to whom the rest of the figures point and on whom they depend. To the left is St Barbara. She, Margaret and Catherine were venerated in the later medieval period as virgins who suffered torture and death rather than compromise their purity and devotion to Christ. To Mary's right is Martin of Tours, a monk and bishop of the fourth century and a worker of miracles for the poor.

The three figures at the bottom right are also from the original window of 1304: St Peter, vested as the Bishop of Rome, with the model of the Church; St Paul wearing a sword; and St Andrew carrying the 'X'-shaped cross on which he was martyred. Together they remind us of the apostolic origins of our Christian faith.

Here at the East Window our pilgrimage ends. From the West Front to the High Altar, we have travelled through space and time from the outside world to stand looking up at Jesus, surrounded now, as we have been throughout our journey, by 'so great a cloud of witnesses' (Hebrews 12:1). With the saints we can offer all that we are to the service of God in his Son Jesus Christ, and so we look forward to reaching his kingdom in heaven, of which the glories of this Cathedral are but the merest glimpse.

✠

Prayers

Send the Holy Spirit on your people,
so that we, in the company of all the saints,
may praise and glorify you for ever.

Alternative Service Book 1980

O God, who has brought us near
to an innumerable company of angels
and to the spirits of just people made perfect;
grant us in our pilgrimage to abide in their fellowship,
and in the heavenly country
to share with them in their joy.

William Bright

You have made us for yourself,
and our hearts are restless till they find their rest in you:
grant us purity of heart and strength of purpose,
that no passion may hinder us from knowing your will,

no weakness from doing it;
but in your light may we see light,
and in your service find perfect freedom.

St Augustine

May the Lord give you understanding
of his wisdom and grace,
and make you diligent in his service;
May he nourish you in the riches of his Gospel,
and make you to persevere in all good works;
May he keep your steps from wandering,
and direct you in the paths of love and peace;
and the blessing of God almighty,
the Father, the Son, and the Holy Spirit,
be upon you and remain with you always.

Leofric, first Bishop of Exeter